THIS NOTEBOOK BELONGS TO ....

CONTACT ....